Begin each day with
gratitude! Write only three,
for a start. See what
happens with a grateful
heart!

Begin each day with
gratitude! Write only three,
for a start. See what
happens with a grateful
heart!

Begin each day with gratitude! Write only three, for a start. See what happens with a grateful heart!

Begin each day with
gratitude! Write only three,
for a start. See what
happens with a grateful
heart!

Begin each day with
gratitude! Write only three,
for a start. See what
happens with a grateful
heart!

Begin each day with
gratitude! Write only three,
for a start. See what
happens with a grateful
heart!

Begin each day with
gratitude! Write only three,
for a start. See what
happens with a grateful
heart!

Begin each day with
gratitude! Write only three,
for a start. See what
happens with a grateful
heart!

Begin each day with
gratitude! Write only three,
for a start. See what
happens with a grateful
heart!

Begin each day with
gratitude! Write only three,
for a start. See what
happens with a grateful
heart!

Begin each day with gratitude! Write only three, for a start. See what happens with a grateful heart!

Begin each day with
gratitude! Write only three,
for a start. See what
happens with a grateful
heart!

Begin each day with
gratitude! Write only three,
for a start. See what
happens with a grateful
heart!

Begin each day with
gratitude! Write only three,
for a start. See what
happens with a grateful
heart!

Begin each day with gratitude! Write only three, for a start. See what happens with a grateful heart!

Begin each day with gratitude! Write only three, for a start. See what happens with a grateful heart!

Begin each day with
gratitude! Write only three,
for a start. See what
happens with a grateful
heart!

Begin each day with
gratitude! Write only three,
for a start. See what
happens with a grateful
heart!

Begin each day with
gratitude! Write only three,
for a start. See what
happens with a grateful
heart!

Begin each day with
gratitude! Write only three,
for a start. See what
happens with a grateful
heart!

Begin each day with
gratitude! Write only three,
for a start. See what
happens with a grateful
heart!

Begin each day with
gratitude! Write only three,
for a start. See what
happens with a grateful
heart!

Begin each day with
gratitude! Write only three,
for a start. See what
happens with a grateful
heart!

Begin each day with gratitude! Write only three, for a start. See what happens with a grateful heart!

Begin each day with
gratitude! Write only three,
for a start. See what
happens with a grateful
heart!

Begin each day with gratitude! Write only three, for a start. See what happens with a grateful heart!

Begin each day with
gratitude! Write only three,
for a start. See what
happens with a grateful
heart!

Begin each day with
gratitude! Write only three,
for a start. See what
happens with a grateful
heart!

Begin each day with gratitude! Write only three, for a start. See what happens with a grateful heart!

Begin each day with gratitude! Write only three, for a start. See what happens with a grateful heart!

Begin each day with
gratitude! Write only three,
for a start. See what
happens with a grateful
heart!

Begin each day with gratitude! Write only three, for a start. See what happens with a grateful heart!

Begin each day with
gratitude! Write only three,
for a start. See what
happens with a grateful
heart!

Begin each day with gratitude! Write only three, for a start. See what happens with a grateful heart!

Begin each day with
gratitude! Write only three,
for a start. See what
happens with a grateful
heart!

Begin each day with gratitude! Write only three, for a start. See what happens with a grateful heart!

Begin each day with
gratitude! Write only three,
for a start. See what
happens with a grateful
heart!

Begin each day with
gratitude! Write only three,
for a start. See what
happens with a grateful
heart!

Begin each day with
gratitude! Write only three,
for a start. See what
happens with a grateful
heart!

Begin each day with gratitude! Write only three, for a start. See what happens with a grateful heart!

Begin each day with
gratitude! Write only three,
for a start. See what
happens with a grateful
heart!

Begin each day with
gratitude! Write only three,
for a start. See what
happens with a grateful
heart!

Begin each day with
gratitude! Write only three,
for a start. See what
happens with a grateful
heart!

Begin each day with
gratitude! Write only three,
for a start. See what
happens with a grateful
heart!

Begin each day with gratitude! Write only three, for a start. See what happens with a grateful heart!

Begin each day with gratitude! Write only three, for a start. See what happens with a grateful heart!

Begin each day with
gratitude! Write only three,
for a start. See what
happens with a grateful
heart!

Begin each day with
gratitude! Write only three,
for a start. See what
happens with a grateful
heart!

Begin each day with
gratitude! Write only three,
for a start. See what
happens with a grateful
heart!

Begin each day with
gratitude! Write only three,
for a start. See what
happens with a grateful
heart!

Begin each day with
gratitude! Write only three,
for a start. See what
happens with a grateful
heart!

Begin each day with
gratitude! Write only three,
for a start. See what
happens with a grateful
heart!

Begin each day with
gratitude! Write only three,
for a start. See what
happens with a grateful
heart!

Begin each day with
gratitude! Write only three,
for a start. See what
happens with a grateful
heart!

Begin each day with
gratitude! Write only three,
for a start. See what
happens with a grateful
heart!

Begin each day with
gratitude! Write only three,
for a start. See what
happens with a grateful
heart!

Begin each day with
gratitude! Write only three,
for a start. See what
happens with a grateful
heart!

Begin each day with
gratitude! Write only three,
for a start. See what
happens with a grateful
heart!

Begin each day with gratitude! Write only three, for a start. See what happens with a grateful heart!

Begin each day with
gratitude! Write only three,
for a start. See what
happens with a grateful
heart!

Begin each day with
gratitude! Write only three,
for a start. See what
happens with a grateful
heart!

Begin each day with gratitude! Write only three, for a start. See what happens with a grateful heart!

Begin each day with
gratitude! Write only three,
for a start. See what
happens with a grateful
heart!

Begin each day with
gratitude! Write only three,
for a start. See what
happens with a grateful
heart!

Begin each day with
gratitude! Write only three,
for a start. See what
happens with a grateful
heart!

Begin each day with gratitude! Write only three, for a start. See what happens with a grateful heart!

Begin each day with
gratitude! Write only three,
for a start. See what
happens with a grateful
heart!

Begin each day with gratitude! Write only three, for a start. See what happens with a grateful heart!

Begin each day with
gratitude! Write only three,
for a start. See what
happens with a grateful
heart!

Begin each day with
gratitude! Write only three,
for a start. See what
happens with a grateful
heart!

Begin each day with
gratitude! Write only three,
for a start. See what
happens with a grateful
heart!

Begin each day with gratitude! Write only three, for a start. See what happens with a grateful heart!

Begin each day with gratitude! Write only three, for a start. See what happens with a grateful heart!

Begin each day with
gratitude! Write only three,
for a start. See what
happens with a grateful
heart!

Begin each day with
gratitude! Write only three,
for a start. See what
happens with a grateful
heart!

Begin each day with gratitude! Write only three, for a start. See what happens with a grateful heart!

Begin each day with
gratitude! Write only three,
for a start. See what
happens with a grateful
heart!

Begin each day with
gratitude! Write only three,
for a start. See what
happens with a grateful
heart!

Begin each day with
gratitude! Write only three,
for a start. See what
happens with a grateful
heart!

Begin each day with gratitude! Write only three, for a start. See what happens with a grateful heart!

Begin each day with gratitude! Write only three, for a start. See what happens with a grateful heart!

Begin each day with
gratitude! Write only three,
for a start. See what
happens with a grateful
heart!

Begin each day with gratitude! Write only three, for a start. See what happens with a grateful heart!

Begin each day with
gratitude! Write only three,
for a start. See what
happens with a grateful
heart!

Begin each day with
gratitude! Write only three,
for a start. See what
happens with a grateful
heart!

Begin each day with
gratitude! Write only three,
for a start. See what
happens with a grateful
heart!

Begin each day with
gratitude! Write only three,
for a start. See what
happens with a grateful
heart!

Begin each day with
gratitude! Write only three,
for a start. See what
happens with a grateful
heart!

Begin each day with
gratitude! Write only three,
for a start. See what
happens with a grateful
heart!

Begin each day with
gratitude! Write only three,
for a start. See what
happens with a grateful
heart!

Begin each day with
gratitude! Write only three,
for a start. See what
happens with a grateful
heart!

Begin each day with
gratitude! Write only three,
for a start. See what
happens with a grateful
heart!

Begin each day with gratitude! Write only three, for a start. See what happens with a grateful heart!

Begin each day with gratitude! Write only three, for a start. See what happens with a grateful heart!

Begin each day with
gratitude! Write only three,
for a start. See what
happens with a grateful
heart!

Begin each day with gratitude! Write only three, for a start. See what happens with a grateful heart!

Begin each day with
gratitude! Write only three,
for a start. See what
happens with a grateful
heart!

Begin each day with
gratitude! Write only three,
for a start. See what
happens with a grateful
heart!

Begin each day with gratitude! Write only three, for a start. See what happens with a grateful heart!

Begin each day with
gratitude! Write only three,
for a start. See what
happens with a grateful
heart!